BREAD UPON THE WATERS

BREAD UPON THE WATERS

POEMS BY

Lorene Erickson

Michigan State University Press

East Lansing

♾The paper used in this publication meets the minimum requirements of ANSI/NISO Z39.48–1992 (R 1997) (Permanence of Paper).

Michigan State University Press
East Lansing, Michigan 48823–5202

Printed and bound in the United States of America.

07 06 05 04 03 02 01 1 2 3 4 5 6 7 8 9 10

LIBRARY OF CONGRESS
CATALOGING-IN-PUBLICATION DATA

Erickson, Lorene.
Bread upon the waters: poems / by Lorene Erickson.
p. cm.
ISBN 0-87013-579-1 (pbk.: alk. paper)
1. Family—Poetry. I. Title.
PS3555.R44 B75 2001
811′.54—DC21 2001000315

Cover design by Ariana Grabec-Dingman
Book design by Valerie Brewster, Scribe Typography

Visit Michigan State University Press on the World Wide Web at:
www.msupress.msu.edu/

CONTENTS

1

BLOOD MOTHER

2

MOTHER SPEAKS

3

SIGHTING THE EAGLE

4

A QUALITY OF THE VISIBLE

5

TO LIVE WITH WOMEN

BREAD UPON THE WATERS

1
Blood Mother

Virginia

Virginia, the youngest,
was saved by a Baptist preacher
who spoke to her in tongues so sweet
her thighs melted

causing the Reedy Creek to rise,
West Virginia mud sucking
at her ankles, water lapping her calves,
the Holy Ghost floating

her all the way to Michigan
and the ward for unwed mothers
where the child was named and given
to Lucy, her Christian sister.

Father Unknown
grew practical, farmed a dairy,
and at forty his heart closed
like a tiny fist.

Virginia rode a return bus ticket
to Reedy undercurrents,
married Gault, the postman.
Each year's baby

washes out of her like gravel.
The creek is chest high now.
She has cast bread upon the waters;
it will not come back.

Wool

Our house was still
those days when Lucy
worked the wool.

She dyed old clothes
into goldenrod and plum,
her hands the voices of flowers.

Ivy at our windows
trailed down from sills,
crossed the sunroom floor

up into the hooking frame
and blistered into loops
under her steady latch.

Marian-Frances, my sister dead
at eighteen months, left
her winter coat for cabbage roses,

their inner stems cut
from my brother George's
Navy trousers.

Words moldered in our mouths
as thousands of twists
bound our lives in rugs

for no one to walk on,
Lucy's silence growing,
emptying the frame.

Relatives took the rugs,
too good for daily use,
and rolled them into closets.

George lined the trunk of his new Buick
with roses. My daughter, Lora, kept
the ivy worked against the black

until a Redwood City flood
rotted the burlap. All that love
unloosed.

Marigolds

Marigolds.
Mary's gold.
Lucy's gold, too,
for she planted them every spring,
indestructible
clumps and masses of gold
tinged with red,
full beds of them by the back door.
Sometimes we couldn't shut the screen
without crushing some,
that acrid odor filling the hallway.

The cancer cells bloomed
like marigolds.
Her body smelled like marigolds.

They last a long time when cut,
two weeks, two years,
her hair spread across the pillow
like marigolds.

The Outing

She had the children
all dressed
when she left the house.
I watched her fasten
the red knitted cap
on the little one
squirming under her touch,
the older one turning in circles.
Those poor little fish.

What a squawking of gulls
must she have heard
as she raised their bodies
high over the railing
of the South Street Bridge.

What thin line snapped
as she cast them like bobbers
to sink and rise and sink again,
the red one the brightest
against the black Schuylkill.

What fisherman, what friend,
what host of passion
did she believe was waiting
that she, too, must join

her skirt spreading
in the air like a net.

Georgean

Three years
after you dropped
between her knees,

your mother cut
the umbilical cord,

hurtling you

through roofs
of orphanages
and foster homes,

down past bedrooms,
beyond kitchens,
drifting toward basements.

The school photographer
caught your head,
smiling,
like Cheshire,
your red hair knotted,

your arms knotted
in a Wayne County General Hospital
jacket.

It took a single shot
to stop your fall.

It took
the Detroit Police Department
three weeks
to identify the severed head
in Rouge Park.

(Your teeth and your red hair gave you away.)

Picnickers still find
your fingers
clutching at bushes.

Blood Mother

1937 NOVEMBER

The month begins in no
your oh rolling over his shoulder
like the moon

over the splintered hill
and you are so cold
starkstill in the churchyard

as his hands search
your coat, your sweater, your underpants.
When his penis bruises you

he whispers in your ear
you are beautiful
until you believe

and his sperm
spiral upward through the neck
of the universe.

1

You said, "I will not name you.
If I refuse you a name, you will not exist."

For fifty years and one
we have been submerged stone.

I cannot call out your name;
you will not speak mine.

In this November
you are dying, mother, and I cannot
help you.

2

You give away things
that no longer matter:
jars of grape jam,
photos of the children you kept,
the damaged heart, collapsing lung.

3

Blood surges in your ears
and the hairs on your body
lift and disappear.

Your senses sometimes for days
abandon that dark raft
you float on.

You push
down into yourself
down into a center of light

and the voice you give up
is your own.

4

I met you, mother, once.

I was wearing my Sunday dress and white
shoes. You stood at your kitchen sink
and quartered potatoes into cold water.

I ruined my clothes that afternoon
in Reedy Creek, pretending I could swim.

5

Once, a letter.

"No one here knows. I've had
heartaches in my life. Most
my own doing. . . . don't tell."

6

I want to bring you my daughter
who would touch her hand to your mouth,
bless you with her daughters' voices.

I want to bring you my sons
great sweet men who bloom
in the wilderness of my history.

These children are yours, I want to say.
I have named them: Lora, Martin, Matthew.
They know me
and I know them.

They say my name–
Mother
and Lorene.

I have recorded their names
in the book of family.

I do not stand alone
when the absence of your voice
presses against my chest
bends my marrow bone.

7

See how I have prepared my heart
made it tender
stripped the cord away.
See how I have sliced it thin

spread it across your plate like leaves
in the unwritten book between us
each piece a word we have not spoken
each sound waiting.

Take it, mother.
I do not need it again
until you are done.

8

In my nightsweat dreams we drown.

We are traveling together
at great speed

until the hill curves
away over the moon
waiting in Reedy Creek

and, mother, we fall
through light
through water
until light closes over our heads.

Our hearts punish our bones
with their beatings,
we tear at what holds us down

and our lungs fill with air
one last time   one last time
until we breathe in water

until we are so full we become water
and a great light shines in us.

And you, mother, drown
in your body
and I cannot save you.

9

Some nights when I enter my house
I believe you are already dead.
That through the distances
I will know your death

in a flash of light behind my eyes
or a drag in my foot
a wrench of my bowels
an intractable anguish

and for a moment I stand
burdened with books and keys

and wait for the sign.
It will not come

and it will not come.
Not because you will not die

but because I step into the life
in my house and forget
again forget you are still with me.

As I attend to small things
you will release your grasp

and I will have
no invitation to grieve
no legitimacy to loss.

There will be no perceptible
ease in the earth's weight

no disturbance of constellations
no sharp cut of the cord

no. I will know,
later, when your body is bone and ash
that you were
and you are not.

1989 NOVEMBER

Vandale and Sons carries you
up the rutted road
behind the churchyard

carries you beyond
the headstones of our fathers and mothers
beyond the survivors
named in the funeral card

five sons, three daughters
nineteen grandchildren
one great-grandchild,
two sisters, two brothers

carries you beyond
me and mine

carries you out
beyond the infinity
in which we began.

Send me a sign, mother.
Speak my name.

2

Mother Speaks

Water

I follow my son to the bottom
deep without breath.

His bones in sinew and muscle
turn to marble in my hands.

My daughter knows the ocean.
Brine seeps

into the channels of her ears,
the moon moves through her eyes.

My mother lifts her mother
from the tub, seventy years,

seventy pounds, stone weight
against the heart.

My father's lungs swell in his chest.
He sinks, already drowned.

Again and again
water reclaims us,

asks nothing of us,
not even acceptance.

Swimmer

When you said you would swim
across the neck of Hell Lake,
why did I not fear for you?

Once, your lungs collapsed,
and your baby hands stopped inside your oxygen tent.
I believed I'd bargained you back.

Why, then, did I let you go,
long fish of my eye,
into the water on that blond day?

I sat in the steamer chair
on a friend's dock, watched
you enter the green calm.

It looked so easy, the other shore
a visible measure, trees waiting,
the languorous heat.

After the first strokes,
your elbows pointing out the sky,
I stopped watching.

It could have been my last vision
of you, your breath and life balanced
in the pure focus of movement.

Now, when the pressure in your chest
expands beyond your limits for panic
and you call long distance,

I offer soup recipes and hopes for marriage,
advice for buying a house. These ripples
are hard as survival, difficult as faith.

Mother Speaks the Back Home Blues

Don't you be coming
in my front door

Son, my Son, my Son

with your plastic bags full
of laundry and books
saying

"I need my room again."

Don't you be bringing
your two degrees and no job here
your hungry friends in
for chicken and rice.

Don't you be leaving
your math theorems on the table
wet towels on the bathroom floor
dishes in the sink
your girlfriends' shoes
under the couch
Penthouse under the bed.

Don't you be giving out
this phone number
to long-distance lovers
who call after midnight.

Don't you be prowling
my house at 2:00 A.M.

turning on the lights
dialing up the heat
turning up the stereo
opening cans of Hormel chili, hot.

Don't you be sleeping
until noon every weekend
with a different woman.
Don't you be expecting
me to remember their names.
Don't you be asking
for the key to my car
and drive through five counties
on my full tank.

Don't you be saying
I haven't done enough
haven't sent you to Scotland
haven't bought you
a computer, new suit
Christian Dior shirts, 36 sleeve
stamps to mail your letters
yogurt.

Son, oh my Son

don't you be filling my house
moving my things
walking into my sleep
cornering my mind.

Don't you be telling me
I don't want to learn
I'm not interested in ideas
I'm not well-rounded.

Don't you be pushing me
to hear you.

Don't you be wanting
me to talk when you
want to talk, and

don't you be saying
"Shut up, shut up."

Don't you be wanting
me to expect your voice

to want you here
to need you.

Son, Son, oh my Son

don't you crawl back under
my heart.

5 April

Morning opens
with omens of snow.

My daughter phones from Palo Alto.
The baby is coming.

She pushes Grace Selah,
shining, out toward willing hands.

Three thousand miles away,
I hear her first cry.

At work we celebrate Dan's birthday
with cartoons reproaching middle age.

My husband, my son and I pass the evening
playing cards. My son chides me

for foolish moves. He only attacks
his mother. Later, he rubs my neck.

Wind swirls the promised snow,
heaviest winter in fifty years.

I remember no life before this.
I envision nothing after.

Wild Phlox

Again this spring unbidden
phlox spill their wild
spiky stars through the green
hedge which marks our yard.
We kneel, surprised

that again these gifts come to us
in drifts and masses. We
turn our faces to the bluest sky,
lavender at our knees,
caught between these constancies

more fragile, more faithful
to the earth's turning than any
love we could hold in our hands or hearts.

Amtrack 351

Houses ravel
into wild phlox

beyond tracks cutting
through Mio, Jackson, Kalamazoo.

The smoker car
rolls and chokes

like Robert, rising
to piece together

another morning
alone, each of us

traveling
in responsible directions.

One woman changes her mind—
doesn't want to go to Chicago;

gets off in Niles.

Matt

When will the photos you mail
from Tucson, paper and chemical

illusions of your presence,
slide out onto my kitchen table?

At what point will my touch
vanish into cactus and gray

mountain measuring sky
too immense to be accountable?

I have begun to count absence for dinner,
to confuse your voice

with the settling house,
the furnace rushing on.

In my dream, you tug
at my nipple, but the old response

fails, and strangers in my arms
whisper "It's me. I'm here."

Honey

Today I dropped the gift of honey. My arms
were full of newspapers, a forest of words,
and I felt it sliding down beyond my grasp,
that perfect amber trapped in glass.

Bill Hahn's stamp was on the jar,
but all that spring and summer
bees had labored in the basswoods, thousands
of flights from bloom to cell, stroking
purple for perfect nests, perfect children
fed by the language of bees.

And Bill in his kitchen filled
the jars, the work of his hands
borrowed from those transparent wings,
nature driven to keep in motion.

The jar hit the floor and shattered.
Honey pooled. Such waste.
Those bees will know.

3

Sighting the Eagle

Sighting the Eagle

She said she saw it,
the bald eagle, I mean. In Michigan,
where it wasn't supposed to be.

She was driving, listening to news
of the probable
peace in the Middle East.

We shot eagles out of Lansing,
Kalamazoo, Detroit,
even Ishpeming years ago.

So what was this woman doing
driving down 13 Mile
with her eyes on the trees?

I don't mean to ask
why wasn't she watching the road—
only why was she looking for eagles?

Did she believe sighting
that fierce beak and eye,
head crowned in white feathers,

would raise a lump in her throat,
hold her hostage to the flag,
the riderless horse, Oh say can you see . . .

when it was only a bird
stalled over a Royal Oak strip mall,
off target, losing altitude.

I say, keep your eyes
on the road, woman;
pray for the sparrows.

Somalia

This name, too, falls from my tongue
like ripe fuchsia blossoms loosened
from their stems and drifting

toward the table's polished surface
in a dining room in Philadelphia or Berlin
or at my own bedside.

Somalia, like the others—Bangladesh,
Brazilia, where boys slit their rectums for coins,
Calcutta, Cabrini-Green—sounds far away and lovely.

I find Somalia on a map—a jagged small piece, blue
along the blue Indian Ocean.

Today, on a road near Mogadishu, a father carries
his dead daughter. I am not told where he will bury
this pile of sticks and infested cloth. This is not

the work of men who would line the naked
along the pit's edge and shoot, 2,000 a day,
complaining that the blood, bone splinters, and brains
splatter their faces. This is not Agent Orange, Scud missiles.

In some other month I will open the atlas
to another buffer zone for arms or oil,
another political scavenge, another religious butchery,
another Beijing or Hebron or Sarajevo.

Do I empty my accounts and send my savings
to Somalia or to Bosnia or Beirut or to Focus: HOPE?

Do I give up my life to volunteer in a hospital or to teach
a global tongue? Do I pray?

No. No. I do nothing.
God does nothing. I do nothing.

Those who will die will die. Thousands.
Here is Somalia. Do with her what you will.

Somalia is a fact of the universe.
Somalia is the sound of someone's tongue
in a lover's ear, soft fragrant fuchsia petals, falling.

Interview

He said he practiced
by snapping
thin trunks of saplings

Trees of Heaven planted
on the boulevard in front
of the new supermarket

so that when
he took the throats
of his two sons in his hands

he would hear only
the brittle sound of trees.

Masada

"You soldiers need an enterprise to fill
your sojourn here," so said our general,
when Flavius Silva ordered us to build

a wall. "To halt the rebel Jews when they
come down," he said, "for come they must; they can
not stay against our will, our might, our Rome."

Each heat-oppressed day, we dug and split
rock, piled stones straight and true. And if I stood
to ease my legs and back, I could not help

but stare up at Masada and the sun
to see those Jews disporting in their pool,
defiant in their watch, or taking in

the breeze on Herod's palace terrace step,
well fed on grain and meat, confined in ease.
With lines and measures, Silva meted us.

We sweated, rationed water, scrapped for shade.
Each night we fell, deadweight, in dreamless sleep.
I didn't hate the Jews nor love the work.

I couldn't see the sense, not even when
we'd blocked all passage from the mountain's base.
I'd trained for battle, not for building walls.

Next, Silva ordered us to move a butte,
to haul it grain by grain and pack it down
again against Masada's western side,

a ramp of perfect plane and slope and path
to march upon those Jews inside their fort.
For three hard years we'd held them there, and when

at last, we broke Masada's gate, I saw
the pools of blood, slain women, children, goats;
the men killed, too. I saw their sacrifice.

I saw the knife the last Jew must have forced
between his ribs, how all the granaries
spilled over full, how clear the water ran

which slaked our thirst. I watched their houses burn.
There'd be no slaves for Rome, nor gold nor goods;
nor even sign of glory for the dead.

But on our empty journey down, I stopped
to lace my sandal tight, and, straightening,
I glanced across the plain below. The stones

shone in the evening light, circumference
of duty and fatigue. That wall will last
awhile, I thought, and, too, I have my life.

I'll tell my son about the wall when next
I'm posted home, for he, and his son, too,
should know our service here, and what we built.

Grand Canyon, 21 June

In my first rib-spreading breath
I pitch over the edge

plummet past
the hawk's wing, until

my dizziness passes.
The rocks

keep their place.
I keep mine.

I do not walk the Bright Angel,
four hours down, eight up,

do not raft the Colorado
or lean between

a mule's ears
into the cauldron.

I pace, instead, the well-
maintained path along

the retainer wall,
step back at open places,

tremble for the father
who stands his son on rimrock.

I take three snapshots
of a doe eating grass.

I skim a borrowed copy
of *A Field Guide to the Grand Canyon.*

At the Hopi Store
I buy a tee-shirt

with a Navajo design,
Whirling Rainbow,

and a Canyon mug
made in Taiwan.

I sit in the swing
on the cool porch at El Tovar

drink Coors, look across the lawn
at Canyon reds and creams,

wonder if Tony the Greek
has finished siding my house

back in Michigan,
know myself: safe, untouched.

At sunset I make chuk-chuk noises
to the ground squirrels,

wish I could feed them
peanut butter and crackers.

On TV in the motel I watch
the birth of a beluga whale

at the Vancouver Marine Institute.
So clearly I see

the female circle her tank,
her blood blooming, the baby sliding out,

their easy roll as they swim
the watery cage.

Sculptor

1. The sculptor holds an egg
between thumb and forefinger,

notes its rough shell,
how its umber shadow curves
in his palm.

He raps the egg sharply
across the iron skillet rim

and with one deft hand
separates the shattered halves,

shakes chalaza and albumen
and yolk with its red spot of blastodisc
into spattering bacon fat.

2. The sculptor sketches
the brush mound of elm,
hawthorn, and black locust

into a buffalo
on the Illinois prairie.

The heap lowers its head
and grazes the blue-eyed grass.

A woman mounts its rump,
splays her hands on its hairy back.
Its crimson pizzle glistens.

The buffalo thrusts itself into charcoal;
the woman leaps between memory and hand.

Now, the red fox approaches.

Seascapes

I saw them at the Tate today, Will,
the Turner seascapes.
They are what I remember of you.

"They're Turners," you said.
"I bought these prints with Donna.
When she left me, I kept them

rolled in my mother's attic
for just this place."
And you opened your arms

to the room you'd built
yourself in Cedarville,
each board cut from native wood.

Then you turned your ear
to the Lake Huron wash,
all you ever wanted to hear.

Turner couldn't paint figures.
He never understood the human body.
You never wanted to.

I needed to see them, Will,
to know again something
that pleased you,

to see the pulse of Turner's suns
and feel the reds quicken
the ceiling over

your watery patch of the world,
the place you call
enough.

4

A Quality of the Visible

A Quality of the Visible

When I ask you which dress
to wear to our friends' wedding,
you recall

the one your sister Maggie wore
in her high school graduation
photo, blue with a lace collar.

I think about wild roses.
You put them in your grandmother's Prussian bowl.
Pollen and petals fell through the night.

You said,
"When you look like your mother,
I'll stop loving you."

But I knew already
you saw your own mother's hands
when I brought you the bowl.

Tonight I will wear blue,
and as we bend together
through a room full of flowers,

you will see in me the moment
when our sons were babies,
my face sweet with surprise.

You Look

you look at him
with the love you look
at him with the love in my eyes

you touch him
with my fingers you touch him
feel his heat as he leans
you lick your tongue in the curve
of his throat   I taste the salt

he does not know
it is me he breathes
he sees another body   yours
your hair nesting his hands

when you press him to your breasts
your belly   press his head
between your legs   he remembers
he remembers only the dark moment
knows only his own cells spinning

we are not a part of him
we are the hundred hands stroking
the eyes looking

When You Think of Me, Love, Consider

bush bean blossoms
blue as my eyes

bean energy
fine fuzz, nap
and pointed tips

tender string
flesh and pale
bean generations

the green smell of summer
minerals coppering the water
in your mother's cookpot

the crisp snap
of provision.

Sweet Indifference

You turn the pages
and your sweet indifference
creeps upon me like a sickness.
I become a compulsive eater.
I chew your hair.
Threads of it catch
between my teeth.
I lick your nostrils,
eat at lips and chin.
The solid crunch of your fingers
resounds in my skull.
I separate and crack each rib,
suck the marrow
and gnaw the soft, pulpy ends.
My tongue surrounds you.
Your blood swells my mouth.
No part of you escapes me.
My jaws ache.
I wipe the last running juices
with my hair.
I reduce you to table scraps
fit only
for stinking dogs
and scavenger beetles.

You turn another page.

Fall Garden

Sleet bangs
hail marys on the last
zucchini in our garden,
clatters among the mums.

I brandish in rubber boots
through biting white
blinding our garden to pluck
yellow mum shoutings

for you for you for you
my whither my lover
my stamen my bloom my blush
my steady weather sweet sheets impending.

Opossum

Tonight, that soft animal
with white fur and needle tail

slying along the side of our house
has come from nearby woods

to search for food or warmth,
red eyes tame with spoil.

In the bowl of light you shine,
she stalls, caught.

You touch my face in the dark,
call me "sweet possum."

When Cats Are Missing

put down your cup
your paper

edge out of your chair
open the back door

listen for the absence
of fur

follow any track
away from your house

find if you can
a clearing

you must kneel
put your ear to the earth

if you are lucky
you will not hear

earth's history
shift under you

your patch of ground
will not unhinge   divide

each leafstalk
moves unmoved

the cats
mewl at your wife's knee

your children
play at hide-and-seek

your cup   paper   chair
wait   you can go back

casualties
will be minimal

5

To Live with Women

Fire

Grandma wouldn't let the men
drink whiskey in her Christian kitchen, so

Grandpa and Papa
stayed up by the sheep barn

long after Sunday dinner, singing
songs they half remembered,

and the current of their voices
swelled down night's icy path

to Mama and me, our elbows
patient on the oilcloth-covered table,

waiting for Papa to take us home.
Grandma served us pie and prayed.

When Papa started up the old blue Nash
for us to leave, the engine

caught on fire. Wires shot sparks
and smoke raised fear in the sober.

Papa punched at the flames with his fists
while Grandpa snatched from the air

a blanket and smothered the blazing engine
again and again, his eyes fixed with purpose

as Noah's must have been when he steered
the ark through holy tempest.

Grandma stood by the gate
testifying for the sins of drink and pride;

Mama's face, her coat, reflected fire,
and the snow at her feet was red.

And me, I pulled from Mama's hands
to beat the fire with the men,

to dance the crusted drifts
down to slush. Laughing, drunk with air,

Grandpa and Papa and I threw scuds of snow
into the smoldering engine, over ourselves,

sweating under our woolens,
our faces hot and strange,

whooping like wild white birds,
and all the while

Grandma and Mama, standing
by the side of the gate, not even singed.

Shoes

My heels upturn
on Papa's iron last.

If a man has pride, he says,
he polishes his shoes.

Trash run down their heels
and Papa mends our leather

to keep us good.
A lady, Papa says,

keeps her pants pulled up
and her dress pulled down.

He pounds another nail,
hidden tongues half-laced.

Papa cuts his workboots
to let the cancer in his heel

breathe out.
I tap my resoled shoes

across the basement floor, swirl
my skirt and dance

for nails and secret iron,
oxblood smells and shine.

Admissions

We push ahead in summer heat
to board the Blue Streak.
The guard rail snaps
down, cramps our legs.
Gears rattle us up.
The park flattens into paper.
On the downward thrust
our bodies rise from the seat,
press hard against the metal,
against our hearts,
one hundred and ten seconds.
We do not hold on.

We turn into the St. Joseph Hospital
lot. Shoulders hunched
against the cold, we walk
the steep hill to the entrance,
ride the elevator to five.
A close friend, cardiac arrest,
racked against the sheet,
struggles to grip our hands.
His eyes edge beyond us.
We kiss his forehead
and back away, back away.

Bone Loss

the hygienist says.

And where do they go,
these grinders, these sieves,
these tooth ghosts?

My vertebrae, too, wear thin,
my collar bones unbutton,
my shoulders unhinge and fall.

Mornings I vow to be a better person,
but the days pass. They pass.
I have given away the piano.

Sometimes I believe
our losses wheel over green waters
and spiral down through the fishes
dropping deeper than plankton or benthos.

Here, atoms of bone and ambition
gather to multiply the ordinary,
become teeth again. And hope.

Overhead, I hear the great Blue
breach for crimson krill, or possibly for happiness.

Cabbage

The summer she begins to bleed too much, she admires the orderliness of cabbages in Pike Street Market. Bloody Mary, how does your garden grow? With blasted seeds and worm-holed leaves, and dense green heads all in a row. Each morning she presses her stomach on the left side until she finds the cabbage she cradles in her pelvis. There is no baby under these leaves.

"Who didn't take out the garbage," her husband says to the smell of cabbage cooking. She shreds cabbage for slaw, her uterus a red cabbage sloughing. In her college speech class a pre-med student showed fibrous fragments of babies' hair and teeth, tumors floating in formaldehyde. She was twenty then, had already unraveled two babies, blood blooming like cabbage roses in her mother's sheets.

She dreams she is pregnant, she dreams of babies, lost ones —where is the girl baby? She looks in closets and cupboards for the abandoned, the misplaced. She unscrews a register and reaches into the furnace duct for a head or leg. Like Perfidia, searching for her kittens. Where is the mew, the milk smell? She hungers for cabbage soup, kraut, stir-fried cabbage, sweet and sour cabbage, babies, boiled cabbage, stuffed cabbage.

Dance

It was in the joint
of her left big toe
that she kept him.

His slow plodding
ways, his inner balance
mystified

her. How he never
danced, how he
lowered his head shyly

in her presence,
how many years
he gave her

of quiet, steady
footsteps.

You Ask

What's it like, you ask,
when the arduous uptrail ends and your next step
pitches your face toward your socks, sliding

wrenching your shoulder along the way,
losing your knee, your balance, your bladder
refusing to behave.

How does the spirit keep, you want
to know, when you hurry on
the maddeningly dimming path,

and the wind takes up the notes
you've tried to say, flies names
up out of your hands in your down going.

You won't want to miss a single rock,
not a muddy pothole, not the bolts of pain
as the thrill takes hold in your throat,

as you lean out into flat land,
as the red meadow flowers snag your ankles
and smear your vision, as the pollen explodes onto you.

You stop, calm, at the hem of woods;
you hear the cool rush of sound. An invitation.
Ask me if any of this is true.

The Couple

She strikes her fists
against his chest.

"God, Morrie,
I knew you'd fall—
I told you. . . ."

"Rosie," he pleads,
"let me up.
If I don't get up,
something will be wrong."

Rosie pushes his forehead down
marks his skin
with the prints of her fingers.
Flowers bloom from the whorls.
She picks them.
They turn to ash.

He is old.
Rosie sees her face
in his eyes,
sees herself alone,
stumbling,
with no one to catch her.

She hates him
for the dark cells
that cause him to fall,
for the crumbling bone,

the pity.
She cannot forgive him for the slow leaving.

She pulls him up
from his knees,
this final proposal,
feels his weight against her,
feels his death enter her.

Skates

I have given my skates
to the dark-haired girl

who must try the ice
where willow leaves luff

across the pond and snag
on botches of crust.

Her ankles will nearly
not hold steady as she circles.

She will, in her turn, learn
cinders on the glaze, ice treachery.

When I begin my afternoon in a tropic place
and walk the beach from point to point,

I will imagine her in blue weather,
her chilled fingers wrapping

the laces tight around the hooks.
She will be the girl on skates,

and for a brief year or night
I will remember, perhaps,

the weight and path of blades;
cruel but necessary desire.

To Live with Women

Autumn,
and I think of the time to live with women.

I see them together, their gray heads
leaning through supermarkets
behind quarter-filled pushcarts.

I see them in Sunday restaurants
squinting at separate checks,
counting change,

companions,
the ghosts of their men long dispelled,
the smell of a man washed from their sheets
for twenty years or more.

I see those ladies
buying K-Mart wool to knit afghans,
greens and purples for distant daughters,
yellow, too, for snapshots of great-grandbabies.

They know
they will survive awhile together,
those old women.

It is autumn.
I think of what I must do
about the house, the family,
to prepare for snow,
another hard season.

I wonder what early star to watch for,
what smell in the air,
what overnight changes in the grass
and leaves and me.

What connections must I make
to prepare for the time to live with women?
What friendships must I nurture
to grow into the light beyond
mother and wife?
What women will wait the time with me?

Who will root with me
through seasons of small purpose?

Who will root with me
through seasons of small purpose?

ABOUT THE AUTHOR

Lorene Erickson taught writing and literature in the Michigan public schools and at Washtenaw Community College, Ann Arbor, Michigan. She now resides in Bradenton, Florida and in Oscoda, Michigan. She is the author of two chapbooks: *Seasons of Small Purpose* and *Blood Mother*. Also, she has had five plays staged in Florida and two plays staged in Michigan. She and her husband, Robert, now collaborate in play writing. In addition, Erickson served for eight years as contributing editor for *The Bridge*, an international literary journal. She continues to write poetry, plays, short stories, and literary reviews.